STRANDED!
Testing the Limits of Survival

Lost in the
WOODS

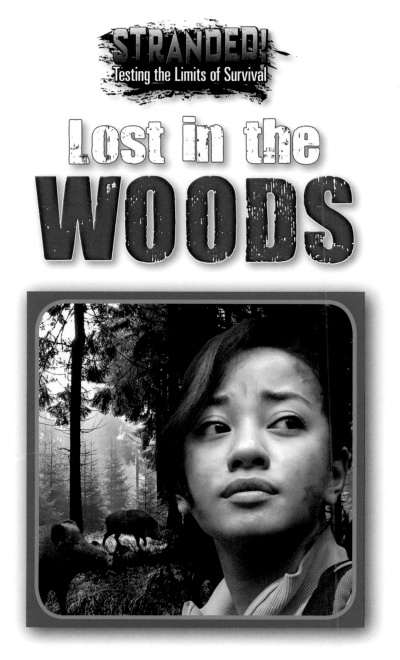

by Meish Goldish

Consultant: Laurel Holding
Head Instructor
Boulder Outdoor Survival School
Boulder, Utah

PUBLISHING

New York, New York

Credits

Cover and Title Page, © bikeriderlondon/Shutterstock, © Val Thoermer/Shutterstock, and © Eric Isselee/Shutterstock; 4–5, © Jim Lundgren/Alamy; 5C, © AP Images; 7, © nikitsin.smugmug.com/Shutterstock; 8CL, © Jason Patrick Ross/Shutterstock; 8CR, © Digoarpi/Shutterstock; 9CL, © Tom Reichner/Shutterstock; 9R, © Tom & Pan Gardner/FLPA; 10, © David Lee/Shutterstock; 11, © Jeremy Penaflor; 13, © Thomas Marent/Minden Pictures/FLPA; 14C, © Johannes Dag Mayer/Shutterstock; 14B, © Stephen Kraseman/NHPA/Photoshot; 15L, © Brian Lasenby/Shutterstock; 15CR, © Rolf Nussbaumer/FLPA; 16–17, © Adelie Penguin/Dreamstime; 17CT, © Handout/Reuters Images; 17B, © Calgary Sun; 18C, © BW Folsom/Shutterstock; 18B, © Brent Hufacker/Shutterstock; 19, © Idaho Sheriff's Department; 20, © AP Images; 21, © RayRay; 22, © Bay News 9; 23, © Jim Culican/Flickr; 24C, © Donald M. Jones/Getty Images; 24, © Leighton Photography & Imaging/Shutterstock; 25, © AP Images; 26, © Cocoa Beach Press; 27CR, © T-Service/Science Photo Library; 27B, © Bay News 9; 28, © Izf/Shutterstock; 29, © Alex Kosev/Shutterstock.

Publisher: Kenn Goin
Editor: Jessica Rudolph
Creative Director: Spencer Brinker
Photo Research: Brown Bear Books Ltd

Library of Congress Cataloging-in-Publication Data
Goldish, Meish.
  Lost in the woods / by Meish Goldish.
     pages cm. (Stranded!: Testing the limits of survival)
  Includes bibliographical references and index.
  ISBN-13: 978-1-62724-293-6 (library binding)
  ISBN-10: 1-62724-293-7 (library binding)
 1. Wilderness survival—Juvenile literature. 2. Survival—Juvenile literature. I. Title.
  GV200.5.G654 2014
  333.78'20289—dc23
                        2014010779

For more information, write to Bearport Publishing Company, Inc., 45 West 21st Street, Suite 3B, New York, New York 10010. Printed in the United States of America.

10 9 8 7 6 5 4 3 2 1

Contents

A Fall in the Woods

One afternoon in September 2013, Gene Penaflor woke up confused and in pain. He was lying on the ground in a snowy forest with a cut on his chin. Gene got up and wandered around. He was totally lost. How had this happened?

Gene Penaflor

Then Gene remembered. He and a friend had come to the Mendocino National Forest to hunt deer. The two men left their campsite in the morning and went to hunt in different parts of the woods. They had agreed to meet later for lunch. While hunting alone, Gene had slipped on steep ground. He fell, hit his head, and was knocked **unconscious**. He had no idea how long he had been passed out. Now he was awake—but lost.

Mendocino National Forest

The Mendocino National Forest, located in Northern California, is spread over 913,306 acres (369,602 hectares). Its woods are popular for camping, hiking, and hunting.

Setting Up Camp

Luckily, Gene was an experienced **woodsman** who often read magazines that give tips for surviving in the wild. He knew if he roamed the forest looking for help, he might become even more lost. Instead, he decided to stay put and wait for rescuers to find him. He set up camp near a stream that he could use for drinking water. Then he built a fire to stay warm.

This picture shows Gene on one of his hunting trips.

Before going to sleep, Gene put the fire out. He knew it was dangerous to let the fire burn all night, since the wind might spread the flames and start a forest fire while he slept. Facing the cold night air, Gene covered himself with dry, dead leaves and grass—or duff—to stay warm.

When he was lost in the woods, Gene often faced freezing temperatures as low as 25°F (−3.9°C).

Gene found a fallen tree, similar to the one seen here, to stay under for shelter.

Forest Meals

Days passed, and no one came to rescue Gene. He was forced to survive in the forest on his own. When he got hungry, he ate **algae** from the stream, as well as berries. He also caught small animals with his hands, including frogs, lizards, and a snake. He killed the animals with a rock.

Gene killed a kind of snake called a brown snake.

Gene only ate berries that he knew would not cause him to be sick.

Gene hunted squirrels, too. They moved too quickly to catch by hand, so he shot them with his rifle. Before eating any of the creatures he caught, Gene cooked them over a fire so he wouldn't get sick from **bacteria** that can cause illness.

It can take lots of time and energy to hunt deer. Although Gene was an experienced deer hunter, he was too weak to hunt the large animals, so he searched only for small creatures.

Squirrel

Lost and Found

Weeks passed, and Gene still had not been rescued. The day he had gone missing, Gene's hunting partner went to the local **sheriff**, who immediately sent a helicopter over the wooded area. Gene heard the helicopter and tried to signal it with smoke from his fire. However, the forest's thick **canopy** of tree branches blocked the pilot's view.

Authorities from the sheriff's department had searched the forest for Gene for four days, on foot and with aircraft. They had to call off their search when a snowstorm struck the area.

Finally, after being stranded in the woods for 19 days, Gene was accidentally discovered by a group of hunters. He was too weak to walk, so the men carried Gene on a **stretcher**. They made the stretcher by tying their coats to tree branches. At a nearby hospital, Gene recovered quickly. His son Gale said, "Trying to stay alive kept him busy, and that is what kept him going."

Gene at the hospital with his family

What Are Woods?

The Mendocino National Forest, where Gene Penaflor became lost, is one of many woods found around the world. Woods are large areas of land filled with many trees. A large wooded area where the trees grow very close together is called a forest. Forest floors are often dark because the thick covering of leaves blocks out sunlight.

Major Woods Around the World

Arctic Ocean

Alaska

NORTH AMERICA

Tongass National Forest

UNITED STATES

Atlantic Ocean

Pacific Ocean

SOUTH AMERICA

ASIA

EUROPE

AFRICA

Pacific Ocean

Indian Ocean

AUSTRALIA

N
W E
S

Wooded areas

Southern Ocean

ANTARCTICA

The largest forest in the United States is the Tongass National Forest in Alaska.

Woods are important because trees allow people and other living things to breathe. One leafy tree produces more **oxygen** than ten people breathe in a year. In addition, a whole forest of trees can **absorb** harmful gasses in the air, such as carbon monoxide. This can help reduce air **pollution**. Trees in a forest also provide most of the wood used to make furniture, paper, and other products.

A forest where much rain falls throughout the year is called a rain forest. This picture shows a rain forest in southern Asia, where North Sumatran leaf monkeys live.

Life in the Woods

Because woods are filled with trees, many animals live there. Some creatures, including woodpeckers and raccoons, make their homes inside the **hollows** of trees. Animals such as bears and beavers also live in the woods. Plants provide these animals with berries, nuts, twigs, and leaves to eat.

Beavers cut down small trees with their sharp teeth. They use trees and branches to build **dams** and lodges in streams. They live, stay safe, and raise their young in the lodges.

A beaver dam

Some forest animals use **camouflage** to hide among the trees. The feathers of the great horned owl blend in with tree bark. Its **prey**, such as mice, cannot see the owl as it hunts. The gray tree frog can change its color from green to gray to brown. Its color matches the color of the tree branch or leaf it sits on, making the frog hard for **predators** to see.

Hidden in a tree, a great horned owl is almost invisible to its prey.

A gray tree frog on a tree

Stuck in Mud

For people who are unfamiliar with how to survive in a forest, things can turn deadly. In March 2011, Albert and Rita Chretien were driving from Canada to Las Vegas, Nevada, when they got lost. At one point, they left the main highway to tour the Humboldt-Toiyabe National Forest. On an **isolated** dirt road, their van got stuck in mud.

The Humboldt-Toiyabe National Forest, located in Nevada and California, is spread over 6.3 million acres (2,549,520 hectares). In early spring, when the Chretiens got lost, the forest can be covered in snow, with temperatures below freezing.

The Chretiens had relied on a **GPS** unit to guide them on the dirt road. However, GPS units are not always reliable in very isolated areas. The information they give can be outdated or incomplete.

Three days passed without anyone coming to rescue the stranded couple. They began to worry that no one would find them. Albert decided to walk to a highway more than ten miles (16 km) away to find help, while Rita stayed with the van. She waited for days, but Albert never returned.

Albert and Rita Chretien

The Chretiens' van got stuck on a dirt road. They could not get cell phone service in the isolated woods.

Running Out of Hope

Although nervous about her missing husband, Rita tried to stay calm. She prepared for a long stay in the forest by trying to make the small amount of food in the van last a long time. Each day, she ate only a few bits of beef jerky, a tiny handful of trail mix, and one piece of hard candy. For water, she drank melted snow.

Rita ate small amounts of beef jerky (right) and trail mix (below), which is a combination of nuts, seeds, and dried fruit.

As the days stretched into weeks, Rita filled her time by taking walks and reading books. She also kept a diary that described what she did each day. By May, nearly two months after becoming lost, Rita had run out of food—and hope. She was getting weaker and weaker. Rita circled May 6 in her diary, believing that was the day she would die if no one rescued her.

Rita wrote notes to anyone who might find them. This note begins, "Please help. Stuck since March 19. No food . . . . Lost my way. Al went to get help."

When the Chretiens first became lost, their family contacted a sheriff's department. However, no one knew the two had traveled so far from the main highway. Authorities focused their search hundreds of miles away from where the couple got stuck.

A Tragic End

When May 6 arrived, good luck came with it. Three hunters, passing through the area on vehicles called **ATVs**, noticed the Chretiens' van. They saw Rita inside, weak and barely conscious. The hunters drove several miles away until they got cell phone service. Then they called 911. Rita was soon flown by helicopter to a hospital. Although she had lost 30 pounds (14 kg) while she was stranded, she soon recovered. One of Rita's doctors described her forest survival of 49 days as "a miracle."

Rita's son, Ray, and his wife, Jennifer, held a news conference at the hospital where Rita was brought.

Sadly, Albert was not as lucky. More than a year later, his body was finally found on the dark, snowy forest floor, about seven miles (11.3 km) from where the van had gotten stuck. Albert had died from **hypothermia**. Lost in the freezing woods, he never found his way to the highway.

This area is near the forest where Albert's body was found.

Albert was hiking in the forest at a time of year when the snowdrifts can become several feet deep.

An Adventure Gone Wrong

A dangerous situation can be even scarier when children get lost in the woods. One afternoon in March 2013, Aubrey Shaffer, age 9, her sister Grace, 6, and their neighbor, 13, were playing outside the Shaffers' home in Florida. They were supposed to stay in the front yard. However, they wandered off to some woods two miles (3.2 km) away after hearing there might be horses on a trail in the area.

Grace (center) and Aubrey (right) with their mother

When they got to the trail in the woods, the girls were disappointed. There weren't any horses. As the sun began to set, the woods grew darker and colder. The girls realized they didn't know the way home. They were completely lost.

The woods where the girls got lost

The girls walked to woods in the Tenoroc Fish Management Area, a place where many people come to fish, watch birds, and ride horses.

Calling For Help

Standing in the dark woods, the girls suddenly heard what sounded like a wild hog. They were terrified! Wild hogs sometimes attack and harm people. Back home, their parents were also scared. They feared the girls had been kidnapped.

Dangerous animals, such as wild hogs and alligators, live in parts of the Tenoroc woods.

Wild hog

Alligator

The parents were relieved when the 13-year-old called her father to tell him they were in the woods. In no time, authorities from the local sheriff's department sent out a helicopter and roamed the woods with search dogs. The three girls could hear the helicopter, but they realized it was flying in the wrong direction. Unfortunately, the teenager's cell phone battery died. The girls needed to think of a way to let the searchers know exactly where they were.

Many police departments use search dogs like this one to look for people who are lost. Some dogs can smell a person half a mile (0.8 km) away.

A Light in the Dark

In **desperation**, Aubrey took out her own cell phone. She thought it was programmed only for games and music and couldn't be used to make calls. Luckily, she discovered the phone could dial one number—911. A police officer on the phone told her to make loud noises to attract the rescuers. When that didn't work, Grace banged her light-up sneakers together so they flashed in the dark.

Grace holds the sneakers that she made light up in the dark.

After hours of searching, authorities finally found the girls with the help of **infrared equipment**. The rescuers then flew them home by helicopter. "It was a huge relief," said Aubrey and Grace's mother. "I was ready for them to run to my arms." The girls were lucky to be found, and their experience is an important lesson. When people go into the woods, they should tell someone beforehand. It can mean the difference between life and death.

A wolf being viewed through infrared equipment

With infrared equipment, people or animals that have high body temperatures appear in bright colors. This helps them stand out against anything with a low temperature, such as trees and rocks.

Aubrey (left) and Grace (right) sit with rescuers from the local sheriff's department.

Woods Survival Tips

If you plan to visit the woods, follow these tips to help you survive.

☑ Before going, study a map of the area. Plan routes to the places you will visit.

☑ Tell people where you will be going and when you plan to return.

☑ Bring a cell phone with extra batteries, but be aware that remote areas of the woods may not have cell phone service.

☑ Pack the clothing you will need to stay warm or cool, depending on what the weather will be like in the woods. Have bright clothing to put on so a rescue helicopter can spot you more easily in case you get lost.

People who take a trip into the woods should wear bright clothes and pack the proper gear.

Bring matches and lighters to start a fire, to stay warm, or to signal people that you need help.

 When building a signal fire, clear a large area of land and start the fire far from trees so you don't start a forest fire. To create a lot of smoke, burn sticks, branches, and green leaves.

 Bring extra supplies of food and water, as well as a small first-aid kit, in case you get stranded.

 Bring a compass to help you know the direction in which you are headed.

 For protection from rain, wind, and snow, build or find a shelter, such as a large log to crawl under.

Supplies for a trip in the woods may include water, food, a flashlight, and a first-aid kit.

Glossary

absorb (ab-ZORB) to soak up

algae (AL-jee) tiny plantlike things that grow in water or on damp surfaces

ATVs (AY-TEE-VEEZ) letters that stand for *all-terrain vehicles;* vehicles designed to travel over rough ground

bacteria (bak-TEER-ee-uh) tiny living things that can only be seen with a microscope; some bacteria keep humans and animals healthy; some bacteria cause disease

camouflage (KAM-uh-flahzh) coloring or covering that makes animals, people, and objects blend into their surroundings

canopy (KAN-uh-pee) the top layer of leaves and branches in a forest

dams (DAMZ) structures made up of a strong wall built across a river or stream to hold back water; beavers build dams to create ponds, where they build their homes

desperation (dess-puh-RAY-shuhn) hopelessness; willing to do anything to fix an urgent situation

GPS (JEE-PEE-ESS) letters standing for *Global Positioning System;* a device that uses satellite signals to provide travelers with directions

hollows (HOL-ohz) empty spaces inside something, such as a tree

hypothermia (*hye*-poh-THUR-mee-uh) a condition in which a person's body temperature becomes dangerously low

infrared equipment (in-fruh-RED ih-QWIP-ment) devices that can improve vision in the dark by making warm objects stand out in different colors compared to cool objects

isolated (EYE-suh-*lay*-tid) far away from settlements of people

oxygen (OK-suh-juhn) a colorless, odorless gas needed for breathing

pollution (puh-LOO-shuhn) materials that damage the air, water, or soil

predators (PRED-uh-turz) animals that hunt and eat other animals

prey (PRAY) animals that are hunted by other animals

sheriff (SHAIR-if) the person in charge of enforcing laws in part of a state

stretcher (STRECH-ur) a long, flat device used for carrying a sick or injured person

unconscious (uhn-KON-shuhss) not awake, often as the result of an illness or accident

woodsman (WUDZ-muhn) a person who lives, visits, or works in the woods

Bibliography

Angier, Bradford. *How to Stay Alive in the Woods: A Complete Guide to Food, Shelter, and Self-Preservation—Anywhere.* New York: Black Dog & Leventhal (2001).

Griffith, Cary J. *Lost in the Wild: Danger and Survival in the North Woods.* St. Paul, MN: Borealis (2006).

McPherson, John, and Geri McPherson. *Ultimate Guide to Wilderness Living: Surviving with Nothing but Your Bare Hands and What You Find in the Woods.* Berkeley, CA: Ulysses (2008).

Read More

Llewellyn, Claire. *Forests (Habitat Survival).* Chicago: Raintree (2013).

Lock, Deborah, and Lorrie Mack. *Forest (Eye Wonder).* New York: Dorling Kindersley (2004).

Tagliaferro, Linda. *Explore the Deciduous Forest (Fact Finders: Explore the Biomes).* Mankato, MN: Capstone (2007).

Learn More Online

To learn more about surviving in the woods, visit
www.bearportpublishing.com/Stranded!

Index

About the Author

Meish Goldish has written more than 200 books for children. His book Disabled Dogs *was a Junior Library Guild Selection in 2013. He lives in Brooklyn, New York, near the woods in Prospect Park.*